Poetic Messages

Poems To Inspire Every Heart

Milton Anthony Green

Table of Contents

Acknowledgements..ix

Preface xi

I Promised 13

Thank You Lord 14

God's Love 15

I Love Jesus..17

I Love Jesus Because 18

My Birthdays 19

A Soldier 20

Be Holy 21

Nothing New Under The Sun...22

Food For Thought 23

Do The Work..25

The Harvest 26

One God 27

Holy Trinity..28

Mystery Of The Trinity...29

Old Story...30

There's No Other God, But Jehovah..........................31

I Know A Man...33

Child Of A King..34

I'm A Fan Of Jesus...35

The God Man...36

Jesus Christ, The God Man..37

Creator Of Variety..38

Potter And Clay...40

Our World..41

Salvation In Jesus Alone...42

My Savior..43

My Shepherd..44

Clear And Simple Choice..45

Heaven..46

A Place...47

Choose..48

Hell...49

Celebration...50

Promises..51

A Question Was Asked..52

Great Tribulation..53

More On Great Tribulation 54

Temptation 55

Too Late 56

Cast Your Burdens 57

Faith 58

My Eyes 59

I Can See Jesus...60

My Eternal Destiny 61

Thy Word 62

Thy Word / It Is Written...63

Where's The World Headed...64

My Adversary 65

The Lord..66

Spirit and Flesh 67

Pretty And Ugly 68

Pray 69

Love My Neighbor..70

Retaliation 71

A Rhyme In Time For My Valentine 72

Virtuous Woman 73

D-E-S-T-I-N-Y..74

Mother's Day Tribute..75

Cambria Heights Gospel Chapel 30th Anniversary......................76

Farewell To Sisters Amy And Lorraine 77

Praise God 78

The Church 79

Thanks Jesus 80

I Remember (Good Friday) 81

Calvary 82

Resurrection Day 83

Salvation 85

Jesus Is Coming Again 86

Repent 87

Prayer For Sinners 88

Acknowledgements

This book is dedicated to all the members of Cambria Heights Gospel Chapel in Queens, New York, who over the years have viewed my Spiritual Gift and encouraged me to write this book.

I would especially like to thank my Elder, Dr. Anthlone Wade and his wonderful wife Jennifer for their valuable support in making this project a reality.

Thanks also to Audrey Bonner, Sophia Russell, Tristan Gorousingh, my dear wife Derron, daughter Lashonda and grand daughter Jayda for their support, time and patience.

Above all I thank God for His inspiration, gift and guidance.

Preface

The seventy poems on these pages were inspired by the leading of the Spirit. They were written as an inspiration to every heart—enlightenment to those walking in darkness and encouragement to those walking in the light.

This World has become more dread! Many Believers because of hardship are drifting away from the Truth and Unbelievers are falling deeper into darkness—The Devil is having a ball!

My hope is that these seventy inspirational poems will help put an halt to this very serious problem— enlighten, encourage every reader and direct or redirect them to the Truth.

I Promised

Two Thousand and Four
I Promised to do more
For Him who died and lives forevermore.
A gift I'm in need
I stayed on my knees
God answer prayers for sure.

A gift to communicate
Things about my Faith
About a God who's Mighty and Great.
To a world without sight
I can help shine the light
With poems He inspires me to write.

Thank You Lord

Thank You Lord for the privilege this day,
Of ministering to people in this very special way;
Providing good food to both saved and unsaved,
For Your Word Dear Lord is worthy to be craved!

Thank You Lord for my spiritual gift!
I'll use it with Honor to give all men a lift.
I promise to use it so those with blindness may see
And to encourage those who believe on Thee.

Thank You Lord for Your Word so dear,
The Spirit's illumination that makes it clear.
Thank You Lord, Your Word I can share;
Thank You Lord for Your every care!

God's Love.

The love that Jesus has for me,
Is the greatest attribute of His personality;
That He should come down and die to save me,
Is still incomprehensible in Two Thousand and Three.

My Lord, My God, out of love He created me;
Then put me on display for all to see.
But deep inside me there was no good;
Always disobedient, not doing the things God said I should.

The term for this is known as sin;
It separates me from God and brings death within.
I too like sheep had gone astray,
Having turned to my own way.

The love of God has brought me back;
Now I strive to remain on track.
But just in case I get derailed,
I'll confess my sins and prevail.

It was Love that laid salvation's plan;
Christ was to suffer and die to redeem man.
Oh what a Savior that He died for me,
On that Old Rugged Cross at Cal-va-ry.

His love's unconditional and it's true;
Christ gave His life to save me and you.
Oh see Him hanging on a tree,
His life blood shed for you and me.

God's love gives me the vic-to-ry,
From sin and death He has rescued me;
I once lived in slavery, but now I'm free;
Saved for all c-tcr-ni-ty.

God's love so deep with width and length;
I can't begin to imagine what Christ underwent.
Why my Creator should love and die for me?
Remains incomprehensible still in Two Thousand and Three;
It was love, not the nails, that held Him to the tree!

Truly, once I was blind but now I can see;
The results of a great love story between my Savior and me;
The Light of this world came and opened my eyes;
And all that remains now, is to meet and greet Him in the sky.

I Love Jesus

I love Jesus for He first loved me;
He's my Creator and Savior you see;
He made me from clay,
Then saved me one day,
For this I'm grateful in everyway!

I love Jesus for He first loved me;
He removed my blindness and caused me to see.
He came knocking on my heart's door;
Telling me how to sin no more;
I took heed of His Words for sure,
Now life is far better than before!

I love Jesus for He first loved me;
He keeps me from harm and danger you see!
There's no one like Him,
To keep me from sin,
Thanks to His Holy Spirit who dwells within.

I love Jesus for He first loved me;
He satisfies all my needs you see;
He sustains and provides,
In Him I can confide;
Nothing can divide,
For He saves, He keeps and satisfies!

I Love Jesus Because

I love Jesus because He first loved me;
While in bondage, He came and rescued me;
Emancipated, I'm full of glee!
Because of His works at Calvary.

He paid the penalty for all my sins;
This isn't the way it should've been!
But thanks be to God for sending Him;
At both sin and death, I'm able to grin.

He abides in me, I abide in Him;
He placed His Holy Spirit within;
To deliver me from the power of sin;
Satan's defeated!, can no longer win!

I love Jesus because He first loved me!
He saved, He keeps and satisfies me!
Without Him, I knew where I was destined to be!
Thank you Lord Jesus for Calvary!

My Birthdays

September, Nineteen Fifty Six, I was born on earth;
Christmas, Nineteen Ninety Four, I had my second birth.
Thirty eight years of slavery, then God delivered me;
Now I pledge allegiance to the one who died and set me free.

Thirty eight years of slavery is a very long, long run;
Living in disobedience, I thought I was having fun.
Then Jesus came to me that day and turned my life around;
He pardoned me and set me upon redemption ground.

Jesus is the Way, the Truth and Life indeed;
He promised to provide me with everything I need.
Only thing I have to do, is do His blessed will;
And promises He made to me, He always will fulfill!

For this I'm extremely grateful, a second chance at last;
He promised to erase everything about my past.
Transformation is the process He tells us all to do;
Just pray and read His Word and He'll guide us through.

A Soldier

I was a soldier in America,
Land of the Brave and Free;
Now I'm a soldier in the Army
Of the one who died for me;
A soldier, A soldier, with much humility;
Serving a Living Savior with all sincerity!

Jesus is Commander-in-Chief,
He sounds the battle cry.
He leads me by His Spirit
And I never ask Him why;
For a soldier never argues,
Nor ask the reason why;
A soldier's job is just to do,
Whether he lives or dies!

To live or die for Jesus,
Is all about the same;
It's written in the Epistles,
To live or die is gain;
A soldier in Jesus Army,
I make no claim to fame;
For each and everything I do,
Is done in Jesus name!

Be Holy

"Be holy, for I Am Holy!"
A command God gave to me;
At first it sounded impossible,
Til the Spirit illumined me.
Notice, God did not ask
But with all authority tell;
How could I forget my Jesus does all things well!

"For without Me, you can do nothing;"
That's what my Savior say!
How can you be holy,
Unless I help you in everyway!
Just yield yourself to Me
And holy you'll be!
Remember, I'm the One who gives Victory.

Nothing New Under The Sun

"There's nothing new under the sun!"
Wise words spoken by King Solomon;
After a sinful life of lust and fun,
Like many before him already done,
Came to realize true life hadn't begun.

He said, "all is vanity," now don't you see;
That's not how life is supposed to be!
Open the Good Book, look and see,
How our Creator intended it to be.

"Be holy, for I Am Holy!"

Food For Thought

The eve before the new year, we meet in God's house;
Awaiting the passing of the old, arrival of the new;
Looking now the year in review;
Consider this thought even as I do;
Did you do enough for Jesus, knowing all He's done for you?

Two Thousand and Three is quickly passing,
Two Thousand and Four almost here;
What if Jesus should appear on the first day of the year?
Are you ready to meet Him without any doubt?
Ever considered the possibility you may not hear the shout?

These thoughts you must ponder each day til the end;
Your labor must never cease til Christ come again.
The harvest is plentiful, but laborers are few;
Trust in the Lord and your strength He'll renew.

So many souls are out there, still in their sin;
In Two Thousand and Three, how many souls did you win?
For Two Thousand and Four let's endeavor to do more,
Not winning one soul, but a minimum of four!

Saved to serve, what I often hear;
Watching some of my brethren, haven't seen that in years!
Salvation, is not just about escaping Hell,
For God commissioned us to go out and tell.
They keep all they know and share with no one;
They'll be surprised to know there's no lone ranger Christian!

Food for thought as we approach Two Thousand and Four;
There's much work to be done, even more than before.
Saved to serve, so serve til the end;
From Jesus you'll hear, "well done My faithful friend!"

Make now your resolution for Two Thousand and Four;
That for Jesus your Savior you'll do lots more.
The sign of the times tell us each day,
Christ coming again is closer, not far away.
To the work, to the work and ponder no more,
Those food for thought, I pose to you before.

Do The Work

Do the work, do the work, in Two Thousand and Four;
We must work harder now, unlike before!
The whole world is in fear, Jesus coming is near;
Do the work, Do the work, we have no time to spare!

There's a whole lot to do;
Yes, there's something for you!
So work let us view
The gift the Spirit has given you!

No more time to lurk,
Let's all do the work!
Remove that smirk,
Please get yourself perked!

Do the work, do the work, a whole lot more;
That's a promise to keep for Two Thousand and Four!
Do the work, do the work, unlike before;
From your Savior you'll receive a crown for sure!

The Harvest

"The harvest is plentiful, laborers are few;"
Don't you hear your Savior speaking to you?
If you haven't a clue, what you're suppose to do;
You're not allowing the Spirit to work in you!

Wake up now from your sleep and slumber!
Don't you know that your days are numbered;
This world has become more dread;
You haven't done much of what Jesus said!

You have become too complacent;
Forgetting first and second greatest commandments!
Someone once witnessed to you;
Do the same for your neighbors too!

Start now before it's too late!
Too many people are lined up for Hell's gate;
You've been commissioned to go spread the Faith;
Do it now and don't procrastinate!

"The harvest is plentiful, laborers are few;"
Concentrate on what you're suppose to do!
Remembering these words Christ said to you;
"As the Father sends Me, so send I you!"

One God

Know the Truth and you'll be free;
Words of the Savior directed at me;
"Trust in God also trust in Me,
The Great I AM, that's who I be!"

He's Creator of Heaven and Earth;
Mankind in the Garden, He did insert;
From the first man came a variety,
Of all the people in society!

He's God of the Colored, Red, Yellow and White;
So why on earth do God's creatures fight?
They've rejected the Truth and did not come to the Light!
Now spend each day fighting for Civil Rights.

They're blinded by darkness and cannot see,
That Jesus died for them as well as me!
If they'll turn to the Light, they'll see;
There's only one God, no matter what color you be!

Holy Trinity

Father, Son and Holy Ghost,
Thou Art Three in One God I love the most!
There's no other God to compare with Thee,
For there's no other God who could've set me free!

Thou Art Alpha and Omega, the Beginning and the End!
Thou Art Creator, Savior, Emancipator and Friend!
Thou Art Lord, Thou Art Life, Thou Art Everything to me!
Thou Art the Only True God who gives victory!

Since my salvation, I've worshipped Thee;
Not Three Gods, but One in Three!
Remainder of life, Thou will forever be;
The Great Jehovah, One God, Holy Trinity!

Mystery Of The Trinity

Do we fully understand the Holy Trinity?
It's defined as one God existing in three;
With our finite minds we're unable to see,
Just how this fact could ever be.

To all, this is a great mystery;
The concept of one God existing in three!
By faith, accept it and one day you'll see,
The great mystery surrounding the Holy Trinity!

Old Story

There's a story from days of old,
To every generation it has been told;
Took thirty eight years, now I am sold;
Repented of my sins, before I got cold!

It tells of a Savior from Glory you see;
His coming to earth to save a sinner like me;
He came as the Light, to show men the right,
Their eyes were opened, yet they lacked sight.

He's a God of Love, Mercy and Grace;
One who was willing to take my place!
It was me who should've been on that tree,
On Golgotha's Hill, at Calvary.

He redeemed me not with silver or gold,
But with His precious blood, the story is told;
His cleansing blood still prevails today;
Just open His Word and He'll show you the way.

I thank God for Salvation brought my way;
To Him only I praise, worship and pray;
Receive Him now while your heart still beats,
For it's too late, when you're under six feet!

There's No Other God, But Jehovah!

There's no other God but Jehovah!
He created the heavens, earth and sea;
There's no other God but Jehovah!
Moreover, He created me!
There's no other God but Jehovah!
He sent His Son for me!
There's no other God but Jehovah!
He set the captives free!

There's no other God but Jehovah!
He caused the blind to see!
There's no other God but Jehovah!
He's the only God for me!
There's no other God but Jehovah!
I'll forever worship thee!
There's no other God but Jehovah!
One God in Trinity!

There's no other God but Jehovah!
He washed away my sins!
There's no other God but Jehovah!
Placed His Holy Spirit within!
There's no other God but Jehovah!
He keeps me free from sin!
There's no other God but Jehovah!
I belong only to Him!

There's no other God but Jehovah!
He tore the bars away!
There's no other God but Jehovah!
I speak with Him everyday!

There's no other God but Jehovah!
He keeps me from day to day!
There's no other God but Jehovah!
I hope to see Him one day!
There's no other God but Jehovah!
I love you Lord I'll say!
There's no other God but Jehovah!
With Him forever I'll stay!

I Know A Man

I know a Man, born a baby in a manger!
I know a Man, existed before as Creator!
I know a Man, came to earth as Savior!
I know a Man, fears no danger!
I know a Man, dislikes a lone ranger!
His name is Jesus!

I know a Man, born a King!
I know a Man, King of Kings!
I know a Man, makes Angels sing!
I know a Man, created everything!
His name is Jesus!

I know a Man, from Galilee!
I know a Man, walked on the sea!
I know a Man, caused the blind to see!
I know a Man, rescued me!
His name is Jesus!

I know a Man, worthy of praise!
I know a Man, raised from the grave!
I know a Man, I fix my gaze!
I know a Man, alone can save!
His name is Jesus!

He can do a whole lot more;
When you let Him in thru your door;
He still does the same as before;
He possesses your every cure!
Him, believers worship and adore;
Helps you to sin no more!
His name is Jesus!

I'm The Child Of A King

I'm the child of a King
These words I proudly sing
Not the child of an earthly king
But the King of Kings

There's only one King of Kings
Another the world can't bring
Unlike all earthly kings
He's Servant to all who clings

I love the King of Kings
He created everything
He leads me in doing right things
All praises to Him I sing

I'm A Fan Of Jesus

I'm a fan of Jesus, He's my Superstar
The most valuable person in the world by far
His stats are real impressive, like Him I wanna be
One who knows no defeat, only victories

I'm a fan of Jesus, best role model today
He's exemplary in all He does, has shown me the way
His game's big on salvation, He died so I'll receive
A far better life to come, when this world I do leave

I'm a fan of Jesus, He takes care of His own
He promised never to leave me, never leave me alone
Has given me instructions, which I daily heed
He tells me not to worry, He'll supply my every need

I'm a fan of Jesus, He's the real deal
He doesn't grant me blessings, based on how He feels
His blessings are a given, it's there for me to claim
After receiving salvation and only in His name

I'm a fan of Jesus, lots more reasons why
Another He's always truthful, He never tells a lie
Promises He made to me, He daily does fulfill
The best of all is yet to come, in the future still

The God Man

Jesus is the God Man,
Another there'll never be!
Sent from Heaven above,
To set the captives free.
He demonstrated His love,
By dieing on Calvary's tree.
Brought salvation to every man,
It's rich, full and free!

Jesus Christ, The God Man

Jesus Christ, the God Man
Creator of you and me
Left His home in Heaven
Come saved a wretch like me
He veiled His glory, deity
As Man He died on a tree
No man took His life from Him
He laid it down for me.

How I love my Jesus
For doing this work for me
Third day was resurrected
Death lost its victory
Sits to the right in Glory
Interceding there for me
A heap of thanks to Him I owe
For life eternally!.

Creator of Variety

Ours is a world filled with variety,
Of everything that exists in society;
Yet one fact remains with us definitely;
There's only one God, Creator of humanity!

View these facts and surely you'll see,
God created a variety of animals, plants and trees!
If one God created varieties in all of these,
Why could He not have created it also in you and me?

There're varieties of waters, oceans, lakes, rivers, ponds and seas;
Varieties of languages, English, Spanish, French, Portuguese;
Varieties of everything natural you can perceive;
Are you saying one God did not create all of these?

We tend to limit God when it comes to the various races;
That from the first man, could not have come such varieties of
faces!
It all comes down to our ignorance and prejudices you see!
Everyone wanting God to look and be the color of he or she!

Regardless of color, God made us from one mold!
Our basic composition is most definitely three fold!
We're all composed of body, spirit and soul!
Proves there's one Designer, I hope you're close on being sold!

It does not take much imagination or intelligence!
All you need apply is a bit of mere common sense!
Look at the basic man, no matter what color he be;
Then take careful notice of every basic similarity!

You should now be convinced there's one Designer of humanity!
Colors and features are optional, Creator's choice of variety!
Other theories or arguments are obviously mere non-sense;
Try using your innate gift of good-old common sense!

Now, are you ready to conclude like me?
That from the first man created came a variety,
Of every race of people in our society!
Thanks to the one God's ingenuity!

Potter And Clay

Lord! You're the Potter, I am the clay
Reason enough for me to love, trust and obey
I strive to do daily all that You say
For without a doubt, there's no better way

You made me for a reason, a purpose too
Show me Lord, all You'll have me to do!
Humble me Lord, fill me with Your Spirit
So when He leads, I'll go ahead and do it

The righteous path is not the easiest of ways
Renew my strength, day after day
Help me stay on course, these things I pray
Never let me stray, just follow the Way
Lord! You're the Potter, I am the clay

Our World

Look at our world, there's so much more to see;
Than corruption, crime, war and poverty.
Look beyond man's sin, observe its beauty!
Everything created with such great ingenuity.

Look at the sky, sun, stars, planets and moon;
Mountains, hills, valleys, oceans, clouds, monsoon.
Ever stop to wonder how it all came to be?
Who created all of this natural beauty?

For everything made, there is a maker!
There's nothing created without a creator!
Nothing originates on its own,
Except for God, yes, God alone!

Skeptics will ask, how can this be?
In times past, this was also me!
I now live my life by placing my faith;
In the Son of God, who I now await.

Special Revelation tells how the world began;
Of all that God created, including man!
Due to hardness of heart, some refuse to understand;
God made it all for His purpose, according to His plans!

Salvation In Jesus Alone

Believe on Jesus for salvation;
Echo these words throughout all the nations!
No matter how vile and desperate your situation;
Jesus alone can give salvation.

There's a task for every generation;
We're to spread the good news about salvation;
Some folks make it their vocation,
Taking it to many different nations.

Time for you to receive an education,
If you'll not accept salvation;
Then Hell will be your destination!
You can't make another reservation!
Til you believe on Jesus for salvation!

My Savior.

Jesus Christ my Savior, He means the world to me;
A loving God and Father, He died to set me free;
In the world, not of the world, that's Christianity;
For only in Christ my Savior, we have the victory!

All my circumstances and all my daily test;
I cast them all on Jesus, He promised to give me rest;
He is truly faithful and will forever be;
For only in Christ my Savior, we have the victory!

My Jesus is Gentle, Loving, Merciful and Kind;
A better Friend nowhere ever can you find;
He's really Faithful, new mercies each morning I see;
And this speaks much highly of His reliability!

Come home now to Jesus, make no more delay;
From any of His children, they can show you the way;
Allow Him into your heart and He'll set you free;
Remember, only in Christ the Savior, there's victory!

My Shepherd

The Lord is my Shepherd, I am His sheep;
He watches over me whether I'm awake or asleep!
He's the greatest Shepherd, no others can compete;
He satisfies my needs from head down to my feet!

There's no other shepherd to whom I'd rather belong;
Most are robbers and thieves, who motives are truly wrong!
They come to steal, kill and destroy, scattering the throng;
The Good Shepherd gathers His sheep and leads them right along!

The Lord will be your shepherd, just come into His fold!
He's the Potter and you being clay He'll forever mold!
Listen and know His voice, do all what you're told!
You'll forever belong to Him and will never ever be sold!

Clear And Simple Choice

Special Revelation,
Tells of a choice of destinations!
Heaven for those with salvation,
Hell for practicers of procrastination!
Time to make a determination,
As to your final destination!

Heaven

There's a place I'm longing to be,
Not in my dreams, but reality!
The Bible speaks of its beauty;
Getting there is my ultimate duty.

A place where the streets are lined with Gold!
A place where you'll never ever grow old!
A place where God lives I'm told!
A place where you can never ever get cold!

A place where there's no corruption or sin!
A place you need not drink rum nor gin!
A place where only Christ can let you in!
This place is known as Heaven.

A Place

A place is being prepared for me,
Where I'll spend eternity.
A House with many Mansions,
One's for me!
From the presence of sin, I'll forever be;
Abiding with Jesus, face to face I'll see;
Accommodations are great,
Rent is free!

Choose

Open the Holy Bible read and know;
One of two places all will go;
To spend our lives in eternity,
Make your choice which will it be!
Lake of Fire, restricted you'll be;
Heavenly places, you're allowed to roam free.

Hell

There's a time coming when sinners can't sleep;
A time coming when sinners will weep.
A time coming when there'll be gnashing of teeth;
Receive Jesus Now before you go under six feet!

There's a real place known as Hell;
Story of a rich man and beggar, the Bible tells.
A place reserved for the Devil and his angels;
Receive Jesus Now and you'll escape Hell!

A place where there'll be a terrible stench;
A place where your thirst is never quenched.
A place where no rain will ever drench.
Receive Jesus Now and you'll be quenched!

A place where there's too much heat;
A place where you can never retreat.
A place where it don't even sleet;
Receive Jesus Now before you go under six feet!

Celebration

Celebration, Celebration,
Lots of jubilation;
Such a sweet sensation,
When Heaven's your destination!

Accommodation, Accommodation,
With high recommendation;
Make now your reservation,
Through God's Salvation!

Promises

Promises, are comfort to a fool;
This is a view from society's school.
Turn to Numbers in the Book Of Rules;
And find the promises of God are cool.

He has never promised and failed to fulfill;
So why not repent and do His Blessed Will?
He has never spoken and failed to act;
So let me enlighten you with some facts!

His Spirit won't always strive with men;
When believers are raptured, what will you do then?
The unrepented, He promises to condemn,
For God hates sin and acts of evil men!

Jesus is coming again very soon;
It could be at midnight or even noon.
Why not repent now, before it's too late?
For He promises sinners won't see Heaven's Gate!

Now, that leaves one place for you to dwell;
Do you really want to spend eternity in Hell?
From what I've heard and all I can tell,
It's a place reserved for the Devil and his angels!

A Question Was Asked

God's Spirit will not always strive with men!
A question was asked, what about women and children?
I explained, when the Bible was written way back then;
The word for mankind, was the word men!

Great Tribulation

There's gonna be a Great Tribulation,
Involving all of the nations;
A time of much devastation,
Especially towards the Jewish nation;
Believe, there'll be lots of speculation!

Before this, the church will be home;
Sinners will be left all alone;
To endure the Great Tribulation,
Where there'll be lots of violation
And plenty of contemplation!

So tell me now, what's your situation;
Why you rejected the God of creation?
The one who also brought us salvation;
Now you're left to suffer desolation!.

Think about this Special Revelation
And about your final destination;
Today make your determination
And receive the God of our salvation!
Or be left in a desperate situation,
So said the God of our creation!

More On Great Tribulation

Special Revelation,
Tells about the Great Tribulation;
There'll be lots of confrontation!
No more mass demonstration,
For that'll be a violation!

There'll be many decapitation;
No probation!
Great devastation!
Just an awful situation.

Here's my recommendation!
Right now receive salvation!
Heaven will be your destination!
There'll be lots of jubilation!

Avoid this awful situation!
No more procrastination!
You'll enjoy the best accommodations!
Only if Heaven's your destination!
Make now your determination!

Temptation

Special Revelation,
Speaks about temptation;
Started after creation,
Caused separation!
Caused eviction!
Spread to every generation.

But, God made preparation,
For salvation;
By demonstration!
There's reconciliation
And restoration,
Thru salvation!

Too Late

When the trumpet sounds and time is no more;
It will be too late for Salvation for sure!
Allow Jesus now to enter your door;
Yes, do it now before the end of your tour!

God speaks daily to every man,
Whether you're rich, poor or Uncle Sam;
Repent right now before you're into a jam!
All Heaven will rejoice including the Lamb.

Now, when the trumpet sounds and time is no more;
Your destination will be Heaven for sure!
From the day you let Him enter your door;
He lives the life, not you anymore!

Cast Your Burdens

"Cast all your burdens on Me and I'll give you rest!"
This says the Lord, why not put Him to the test.
He's extremely faithful, what He says, He'll do;
I've challenged Him at His promises, why dont you!

Be anxious for nothing, only be concerned;
Thru prayers and supplication, blessings you'll earn!
Cast your burdens daily, leave them at His feet!
To trust and obey Jesus, is oh, so very sweet.

My Jesus is ready and able, always in control;
He alone gives the peace, that guards our heart, mind and soul.
So cast your burdens at His feet, leave them all there;
Remember them no more for the rest of your years.

Faith

Faith is a term use in Christianity,
To believe on the things we can't yet physically see;
It plays a vital part in our spirituality;
For without it, God has no meaning to me.

Faith is our eyes when we worship in spirit;
A measure has been given every man as a gift;
All we need do daily is exercise it,
Then we'll become more spiritually fit!

"We walk by faith and not by sight,"
It's the only way now we can walk in the Light!
The day is coming when faith will give way to sight;
Then the unbelievers will know, Christians were right!

My Eyes

My eyes are very important parts of me,
With them many physical things I see.
But when it comes to my Christianity,
It's by faith that I 'm able to spiritually see.

"We walk by faith and not by sight,"
It's the only way now we can see the Light.
Without it, spiritual things are as dark as night!
To the Kingdom of God we'll never have the right!

"Blessed are those who believe, yet did not see!"
That's a blessing extended even to me;
I know one day with eyes, I'll see the Light;
For I'm told my faith will give way to sight.

I Can See Jesus

I can see Jesus, though not physically;
I can see Jesus, yes, spiritually!
It's with my eyes of faith that I see;
Jesus my Savior, He's a reality!

I see Jesus everyday;
I see Him whether I'm at work, school or play!
I see Jesus even when I'm at home;
He promised never to leave me alone!

Do you have Jesus in your sight?
Matters not whether day or night;
There's only one way to see the Light,
Receive His Salvation and make yourself right!

My Eternal Destiny

Destiny, my eternal destiny,
It's a place I can't yet see,
At least not physically;
But it's been promised to me!

Destiny, my eternal destiny,
A place where by Faith I see,
As its been described to me,
Indeed it's a reality!

Destiny, my eternal destiny,
The place I hope to be,
When Christ come back for me;
Then with my eyes I'll see,
My eternal destiny.

Thy Word

Thy word is a lamp unto my feet;
It guides me throughout all of life streets!
It's food for my spirit, filled with meat!
Oh my Lord, what a wonderful treat!

Thy word is a light unto my path;
It shows me God's love and also His wrath!
That any man should perish, He wishes naught!
It points me to Jesus, the Savior I sought!

I love to partake daily of Thy word;
Sharing it with others who may never have heard!
All types of people, including Nerds;
Those who say there's no God, now that's absurd!

Thy word I'll cherish each and every day!
A lamp that shines light along my pathway;
It nourishes my spirit and in truth I can say,
Jesus is indeed the Truth, Life and Way!

Thy Word

Thy Word have I stored in my heart,
So that I may not sin against Thee;
This bit of advice is very precious to me!
For each time the Devil tries to be smart,
I pull scriptures from my heart;
I give him no other choice but to flee!

It Is Written

These three words, "it is written," is another precious gem;
Said before each Bible quote, keeps the Devil fleeing friends!
Jesus used it in the wilderness, remember when?
Still works today as it did back then!

Where's the World Headed

Round and around and around it goes;
Where's the world headed?
Many don't even know!
If they read the Holy Bible, it will show;
It's headed for disaster, its creator says so!

The Word of God is such a wonderful tool,
I pray they'll place it back in the schools!
Teach our children from this Book of Rules,
And the world will be fortunate to have a lot less fools!

The Bible tells the creation story from start to end;
Why not read and share it with a friend!
Then surely you'll come to realize like me,
The world is headed for a catastrophe!

My Adversary

Lord! Your word is the lamp which lights my path;
It makes me conscious of Your impending wrath;
It has cured my blindness—opened my eyes;
It has given me directions—made me wise.

It speaks of my adversary, the father of lies;
Even to this day he alone I despise!
He tricks with half-truths, before you realize;
He has fooled you completely with another of his lies

It speaks of his appearance, the master of disguise;
He's very deceptive, appears in all forms and size.
Thank you dear Lord for opening my eyes;
Your wonderful word has made me wise!

He only does wrong, he never does right;
He's the prince of darkness, he's afraid of the Light!
Whenever he comes, he really puts up a fight;
But I pull out my sword and with it I do smite!

The Lord

The Lord's a present help in times of trouble;
Whenever I'm in danger, He helps me on the double!
His help is for certain, it's closer than near;
With an assurance like this, what have I to fear!

The Lord is my Shepherd, I shall not want;
He supplies all my needs with things others can't!
I need never to rage, I need never to rant;
For Jehovah-Jireh is my supply giant!

The Lord is my refuge in times of storm;
He's also my refuge when times are norm;
He's my shelter, fortress, He keeps me from harm;
He's loving, protective, caring and warm!

Spirit and Flesh

The spirit's willing, but the flesh is weak;
This little phrase many of us do speak;
For the spirit's willing and ready to do;
But then the flesh is tempted, not wanting to do!

This is the reason God wants can't get done;
For the flesh is lustful, just wants to have fun;
The things God wants, the flesh won't let it get done;
So simply allow your spirit to take over and run!

Pretty and Ugly

There's one thing I dislike, it really bothers me;
It's hearing individuals calling others ugly!
Who do we think we are, that we ever should?
Afterall, when God made man, He called His work good!

Who determines pretty or so-called ugly faces?
It sure wasn't God, for He made all of us aces!
We're all unique, wonderfully and fearfully made;
My face for another, I never ever want to trade!

I'm extremely thankful to God for having blessed me;
He never once labeled me pretty or ugly!
Instead I'm the unique person He wanted me to be;
One who loves, praise and worship Him only!

Pray

I wake up each morning and I pray
Oh Lord, bless me in this brand new day
Help me to be strong in everyway
Guide my steps every minute of the day
Help me face the challenges that comes my way
At work, school, home or even at play.

It's a beautiful world, I'm so glad
But things occurring, makes me real sad
All the evil and terror in the world today
It's no wonder I get on my knees and pray.

Morals and true love rarely exist today
The world on a whole have strayed from God's way
It isn't too late to come back to Him
The one who saves and forgives us of sin.

These are signs of the times prophesied long ago
If you read your Bible then you would know
I've committed my life to following the Way
That's why each morning I read my Bible and pray.

I Love My Neighbors

I love the Life
I love my wife
I must love my neighbors too
Whether enemies or friends
I must love them til the end
That's what God says I must do!

Retaliation

When we are wronged, do not retaliate;
Just one of the teachings of the Christian Faith.
It's not at all easy, but at any rate;
Show restraint and love, do not retaliate!

Smitten on the right cheek, turn the left one too;
This is what the Master instructs us all to do.
He lead by example during His crucifixion, true!
He passed on this principle to me and you.

A Rhyme in Time For My Valentine

Darling,
What's better than roses, flowers or even candy too?
These sincere words of mine, telling, How much I love you!
Now, what I'm about to express, is absolutely priceless,
So listen carefully, to all I'm about to confess!

This Valentine's Day, I just want to say,
I love you darling in a very special way!
You're sweeter than honey, more precious than money;
My days no longer gloomy, but instead bright and sunny.

I love you for your beauty deep within
And your walk in the light, abstaining from sin;
Your external beauty I also admire,
So much so it sets me on fire!

You're the girl of my dream, so it seems;
This year be my valentine, next year my queen.

Virtuous Woman

I have a virtuous woman to call my wife;
I have a virtuous woman to share my life.
I have a virtuous woman that's fun indeed;
A virtuous woman who fills all my needs.

A virtuous woman, she alone I desire;
A virtuous woman, she sets my heart on fire;
A virtuous woman, she's there down to the wire;
A virtuous woman, whose love forever I'll require.

A virtuous woman, who walks in the light;
A virtuous woman, I love to have in sight.
A virtuous woman, who never fuss and fights;
A virtuous woman, who knows wrong from right.

A virtuous woman, with external beauty;
A virtuous woman, she's such a cutie.
A virtuous woman, with an attractive booty;
A virtuous woman, who's very soothly.

Destiny

D——E——S——T——I——N——Y
Something we can't always see;
But God not you or me,
Knew we were meant to be;
It's our destiny!

So let's unite our hearts
And give our lives a brand new start;
Only through death we'll part,
Let nothing else divide our hearts;
As this was meant to be,
Our destiny!

Mother's Day Tribute

Mothers, on this your very special day,
This Brethren from Cambria just want to say;
Enjoy your day in every way,
For all of you, I'll never cease to pray.

Mothers indeed are very special girls,
That our Creator use to populate the world;
For after He created Adam and Eve,
Child birth to mothers He then leave.

Not all would have children, you should know!
Child birth's a blessing, the scripture says so!
Be a spiritual mother and you can help feed,
A child of God someone else breed.

If you are barren, doesn't mean you aren't blessed;
Don't take it to heart and become overly stressed;
God in His Sovereignty made you this way,
Pray His will be done, day after day.

Thank all of you mothers for the unique work you've done,
In rearing the children, daughters and sons.
Although it's not over, today rest and have fun;
And let your lights shine as bright as the sun!

Be recognized, encouraged and continue doing great;
Above all remember The Author and Finisher of your faith!
This Brethren from Cambria wishes you all God speed;
As you continue a life long duty of motherly deeds!

HAPPY MOTHER'S DAY!

C.H.G.C. 30th Anniversary

Thirty years ago, October
A little church was born
Planted by few Brethren
Vision and faith, moved on
There was a need, a desire
Cambria Heights Community
Spent hours every day
On their bending knees.

In the will of the Lord
Nineteen Seventy Four
Cambria Heights Gospel Chapel
Opened up its door
Serving the community needs
Spiritually and physically
Giving thanks, praising God
For the privilege and opportunity

It's not a perfect church
Will not claim to be
Preach unchanging Word of God
Equip Saints for ministry
Ever in our neighborhood
Stop in! Salvation's free
Join us as we celebrate
Thirtieth Anniversary.

Farewell to Sisters Amy and Lorraine

Beloved sisters Amy and Lorraine,
If I said nothing today, it would be ashame.
I thank you for your fellowship sweet;
Your hugs, kisses and smiles each time we meet.

The three years I've been here, you've been so very dear;
You've always encouraged me in the same Faith we share.
I thank you for your hospitality, love and prayers too;
How do I know you pray for me? You told me you do!

I now pray the Lord's blessings, on both of you this day;
As in a few days from now, you'll be on your way.
Where ever you go, whatever you do, this I'll say to you;
Continue to acknowledge Him and He'll guide you through!

Praise God

Praise God daily, something we must do
Praise and give Him thanks, for all He's done for you
He's worthy of our praises, honor and glory too
Praise Him for His grace, goodness and mercies to you

The Church

The Church's one foundation
Jesus Christ is head
A living God and Savior
Of others, this can't be said
He's our Chief Shepherd
Paved the way that we
His body, sheep, bride or church
Have life eternally.

Make Jesus now your Shepherd
You will never want
Psalm Twenty Three tells us
He does what others can't
Repent today, join the fold
Enjoy sweet fellowship indeed
The Shepherd, Jehovah-Jireh
Will supply your every need.

Thanks Jesus

Gentle Jesus, so meek and mild;
Thanks for watching over Your little child;
Thanks for Your blessings, daily I see;
Thanks for salvation so rich and so free.

Thanks for the love You've given me;
Now in a different light my neighbors I see;
That not one should perish, but be set free;
That attitude of Yours is now also in me.

Thanks for the hope You've given me;
That one day soon, I'll be and reign with Thee;
Abundant life, You've given to me;
Life with You today and for eternity!

I Remember (Good Friday)

Lord, Today's Good Friday, I remember Thee
As my mind goes back to Calvary
By faith I see You hanging on a tree
As you gave Your life to rescue me

I remember the graphic details of Your death
I hear the people shouting their death threats
How the soldiers parade You through the streets
Then drove those spikes through Your hands and feet

I see the Roman Soldiers having fun
As they tortured God's only begotten Son
Little did they know, this was to be done
The redemptive work had just begun

The beatings You took was so severe
One no ordinary man could ever bear
They beat You so hard, Your skin was rent
Yet You showed no anger nor did You vent

The agony and shame, You took in stride
Nailed to a cross with a thief on each side
With a loud voice, You then cried
Even forgave them all before You died

"It is finished!," the redemptive work is done
The ransom paid by God's begotten Son
He gave His life to rescue me
From sin and death, I'm forever free
Thank You Lord for Calvary
Forever My Savior, I'll remember Thee!

Calvary

Let me tell you all I know about Calvary;
It's the place where Jesus laid down His life for me;
It's the place where the whole world came to be,
Reconciled unto God most definitely!

It's the place where my Savior's blood was shed!
It's the place where Jesus gave His life in my stead!
It's the place where Jesus was pronounced dead,
With the crown of thorns still on His head!

It's the place where the penalty for sin was paid!
It's the place where a thief on a cross got saved!
It's the place where sin power began to fade!
It's the place where God's salvation plan was displayed!

Resurrection Day

Was on Good Friday, that Jesus gave;
His life a ransom, mankind to save;
From sin and death, He set us free;
When He died on Calvary's tree;
His accusers hope this was the end;
But Jesus would live to reign again!

Following His death on the tree;
A disciple asked Pilate for the body;
He prepared and buried it in a tomb;
Somewhere inside the earth's womb;
While Jesus body laid there alone;
The entrance was sealed with a very large stone;

Guards were posted at the scene;
Makes one wonder what does this mean?
Was His accusers, who made such appeal;
To ensure Christ's body no one could steal;
Wasn't that they ever cared;
But His resurrection they really feared!

They remembered all what Christ did say;
"I'll destroy the temple, rebuild in three days;"
Security measures were taken to ensure;
No one could enter or exit the tomb's door;
But it all happened like Jesus had said;
For three days later, He rose from the dead!

Because He lives, we too shall live;
Life after death He alone can give;
For God so loved, that He gave;
His Son to die and be raised from the grave!

Today we celebrate Resurrection Day;
To Jesus My Savior, I just want to say;
You're worthy of Thanks, Honor, Glory and Praise
I worship a living God, not one in the grave!

Salvation

Salvation's rich
Salvation's free
Without Salvation
There's one destiny.

Jesus endured the cross
Despising the shame
Reject Him still
His work was in vain.

Repent of your ways
Be transformed today
Receive Christ as Savior
He's the Truth, Life and Way.

Jesus Is Coming Again

Jesus is coming again
We know how, but we don't know when
Remain steadfast and faithful friends
He promised He's coming again.

Jesus is coming again
Like a thief in the night He'll come back friends
So live your lives holy til the end
He promised He's coming again.

Repent

Repent, Repent!

With men, God's Spirit won't always strive
Why not be quickened! yes, be made alive
You've too long walked the wrong path
You're destined to feel the fury of God's wrath

God wishes all men would repent
That's why Jesus Christ He willingly sent
Into the world to die for all
Hear His voice and heed His call

God does not wish anyone to perish
All who loves Him, He undoubtedly cherish
His Son paid the price to set us free
When He died on Calvary's tree

Come on home, abide in The Way
Repent right now, no more delay
Salvation's rich, full and free
Tomorrow there's no guarantee

Prayer For Sinners

Our Blessed God and Father, we bow in your presence each day;
Hear our cries each morning, even now as we pray!
We pray foremost for the salvation, of men everywhere;
Because you made us special, also very dear.

We know It's not Your wish, that any man should perish!
For You love us with an everlasting love and only us You cherish.
And so You sent the perfect Lamb, Your Son, that He should
    perish;
To redeem mankind from all their sins, for it's us You love and
    cherish.

We know that Jesus is the key in Your salvation plan;
Sent from Heaven above, He came down as a Man!
So that all mankind could know, hear and also see;
The God who created heaven and earth, also humanity.

There's no more time for rejection or to procrastinate!
Jesus will return at just the right time, He's never ever late!
Receive Him now and start, your daily walk by faith;
And you can now be on your way to entering Heaven's Gate.

Father, as this prayer goes up from Your children everyday;
Speak to the hearts of sinners and may them hear You say!
Jesus is coming again and soon without much more delay;
Receive Him into your hearts right now or the penalty you'll pay!